# A Century of Prices

An Examination of Economic and Financial Conditions as Reflected in Prices, Money Rates, etc., During the Past 100 Years, With a View to Establishing General Principles Which May Aid in Interpreting the Present and Future.

**By Ex-Senator THEODORE E. BURTON,**
Chairman Board of Directors Merchants National Bank of New York, Author of "Crises and Depressions," etc.;

**And G. C. SELDEN,**
Managing Editor of "The Magazine of Wall Street," Author of "The Machinery of Wall Street," etc.

FRASER PUBLISHING
Burlington, Vermont

*Originally published in 1919
by The Magazine of Wall Street*


*Fraser Publishing Company Edition, 1996
a division of
Fraser Management Associates, Inc.
Box 494
Burlington, Vermont 05402*


*ISBN:0-87034-123-5
Library of Congress
Catalog Number: 96-84378*


*Printed in the United States of America*

## INTRODUCTORY NOTE

THE chapters and graphs comprised in this book first appeared in The Magazine of Wall Street and were widely commented upon not only for their unusual originality but for the practical bearing of the principles developed upon the actual work of the business man or investor.

History tells what happened, but these graphs, with the keen analyses which accompany them, show *why* it happened, and explain the great controlling principles of business and finance in the straightforward fashion of one business man talking to another.

The authors require no introduction to the American reading public. Ex-Senator

## A CENTURY OF PRICES

Burton is one of the world's leading authorities on prices and their relation to economic and financial conditions, and G. C. Selden is internationally known for his keen and thorough analyses of the effects of economic factors on business and investments.

   THE MAGAZINE OF WALL STREET
August, 1919

## CONTENTS

### Chapter I.

## PRICES AS AN INDEX OF ECONOMIC AND INVESTMENT CONDITIONS

Why the study of statistics is called "dry"—The value of the graphic method of presentation—Interpretation of economic and financial conditions in the light of the past—Importance of prices—Meaning of the money rate—Why the commercial paper rate is used—The averaging of prices—Relation between bond yields and bond prices—The stock average—What is meant by a "weighted" average of commodity prices—The method of interpretation—The permanency of general principles—Inter-relations among the different

# A CENTURY OF PRICES

factors—The influence of wars—The general purpose of these chapters.

## Chapter II.
## GREAT ECONOMIC FORCES SINCE 1790

American conditions alone inadequate for a broad view—Why English prices are chosen—English commodity prices since 1782—Prices as a relationship—The "psychology" of prices—Pronounced effects of wars on commodity prices—Effect of cheaper production—The supply of money—Gold production—World's stocks of gold—Increased use of credit—Minor changes in commodity prices now less violent than formerly—The supply of capital—Prices and yields of British consols—The two main elements in their price level—Growth in the supply of capital—The "flow" of capital—Effect of the accumulation of liquid capital—How more money and credit raise commodity prices—Why bond yields rise and fall with commodity prices—Real income versus money income—Post war price movements—Practical conclusions.

CHAPTER III.

## WHAT AMERICAN COMMODITY PRICES SHOW

Causes of war prices—Effect of currency inflation in the Civil War—Comparison between the World War and the Civil War—Elements in Civil War currency prices—Difference between depreciated and expanded currency—Differing relations with European price level—Commodity prices and our export trade—International adjustment of price levels—How our export balance depends upon relative price levels—Effect of large exports in stimulating general trade—Pronounced influence of

A CENTURY OF PRICES

gold imports—The "major cycle"—Interbalances—Wheat and cotton.

Chapter IV.

## CAUSES OF CHANGES IN INTEREST YIELDS AND MONEY RATES

Relation between demand and supply of capital—Capital is the product of labor—Factors in the supply of capital—Rapidity of circulation of capital—Capital classified according to rapidity of circulation—Importance of distinguishing between fixed and circulating capital—Rise and fall of bond yields—Why higher commodity prices increase the demand for capital—Diversion of capital into fixed forms—The disposition to save—Money rates—Connection with bond yields—Causes of high rates—How over-extended bank loans arise—Scarcity of credit down to 1874—

## A CENTURY OF PRICES

High rates of panic years—Is "tight money" a thing of the past?

### Chapter V.
### PRINCIPLES OF STOCK PRICES
### By G. C. Selden

Relations with factors previously discussed—Rising commodities benefit industrials—How stockholders sometimes profit at the expense of bondholders—Panics affect all securities—The "minor cycle"—Various explanations offered for recurrent declines—The fundamental cause—Action and reaction—Strong and weak buyers—Speculation in trade channels—Mutual influence of stocks and business conditions—Features of the minor cycle—Stocks and the money rate—Bull markets are based on surplus funds—How stocks forecast business conditions.

Chapter I.

## PRICES AS AN INDEX OF ECONOMIC AND INVESTMENT CONDITIONS

THE study of statistics is commonly accounted "dry." Yet it is dry only because dryly presented or imperfectly understood. When statistics over a period of years are made quickly intelligible to the eye by graphic charts and diagrams, and when the great vital and controlling influences which cause the rise and fall of these pictured lines are understood and visualized, the subject becomes more fascinating to the business man than the most "gripping" novel of adventure. In these chapters our effort is to present the subject in this intelligible and practical way,

# A CENTURY OF PRICES

as business men talking to business men, and an elaborate series of graphs has been prepared for the purpose.

The great practical importance of interpreting present and future economic and financial conditions in the light of the past can hardly be over-estimated. In this field it is most emphatically true that coming events cast their shadows before. The prime difficulty in the past has been the lack of adequate records, over a sufficiently long period, of prices and other economic and industrial statistics. That difficulty, however. is being gradually overcome. The completeness and accuracy of current statistics are improving year by year as their importance comes to be more generally recognized; while the painstaking researches of students have shed much additional light on the price levels of the past and their causes. The graphs which accompany

## A CENTURY OF PRICES

these chapters not only bring together in a convenient form the laborious researches of others, but they contain additional matter, which is the result of the patient delving of the statisticians who have assisted us in this work.

Comparative statistics of this character afford a means of determining the trend of events. Rightly interpreted, they give a warning of coming changes which is of the highest significance.*

---

* In this connection it may not be amiss to mention Senator Burton's confident prediction, in an address before the American Investment Bankers' Association at Denver, in September, 1915, that a period of higher money rates and scarcity of capital was approaching —a prediction that was naturally unwelcome, but proved strikingly correct; or Mr. Selden's forecast, in an article published in November, 1916, that the then rising trend of bond prices would culminate early in 1917 and that a considerable decline would follow— also opposed to the views of many bond men at that time, but remarkably fulfilled in the outcome. These instances are mentioned to show that studies of this character, by some dubbed "theoretical," are not without a very direct and definite value.

# A CENTURY OF PRICES

## IMPORTANCE OF PRICES

In viewing economic and investment conditions broadly over considerable periods, prices (including the interest rate—the price of capital) are perhaps more important, and certainly more all-inclusive, than any other class of statistics.

Money rates, for example, are the result of a country-wide and, under normal conditions, a world-wide demand and supply of capital. Nearly every enterprise is a borrower. Every bank, and many other institutions and individuals, are lenders. Every investor controls some fraction of the available supply of capital. Even the small accumulations of savings bank depositors indirectly reach and affect the money market. A general fall in the profits of business men is immediately reflected in their necessity for increasing their loans, while a rise in their profits soon brings an increase in bank deposits and thus larger offerings of liquid capital and easier money rates.

In short, the movements of money rates, when properly understood, afford a sort of combined index to the whole industrial and investment situation, and similar principles apply to the other factors here discussed.

It is important to distinguish between the short term money rate, the longer term rate and the price of investment capital as shown by the average income yield on high-grade bonds. The rate for call money, which is dependent on the immediate supply from day to day, is not broadly indicative of fundamental money market conditions; and to some extent the same is true of time money. The money rate used in the graph covering that field which accompanies a succeeding chapter, is the rate for prime commercial paper, usually of about six months' maturity. This term is long enough to afford considerable stability to the rate, and this form of credit is also most closely connected with industrial conditions. Moreover, it is possible to compile this rate more accurately and from an earlier date than in the case of call or time money.

## AVERAGE PRICES

In dealing with bonds, stocks, and commodities the only way to get a general view is to average the prices of a large number. The price of any one bond, stock, or commodity is likely to be influenced by special causes peculiar to itself. But by averaging a score of the principal bonds or stocks, or a hundred commodities, these minor or exceptional variations are for the most part eliminated, so that the movements of the resulting averages reflect general conditions.

## A CENTURY OF PRICES

In the case of bonds, the computation of such an average is embarrassed by the fact that every bond has a date of maturity, when it will be redeemed at par value. Therefore a bond selling at a discount gradually rises to par, while a bond at a premium gradually falls to par, regardless of the demand and supply of capital. So it is necessary to average, not the price of bonds, but their yields to maturity as obtained from the bond tables (or from the tables arranged in graph form, which are more convenient for most purposes).

This average of bond yields is, in a broad way, the reciprocal of bond prices; that is, its general movements are exactly opposite to those of bond prices, since the higher the price the lower the yield.

A graph showing this average of bond yields over a long period is really illuminating, when taken in connection with

## A CENTURY OF PRICES

similar graphs showing other important economic factors for corresponding times.

Since stocks have no date of maturity, a simple average of the prices of 20 to 50 different issues serves to compare the general level of the market from year to year or month to month.

A similar method is followed in comparing the relative planes of commodity prices at different times. One widely used average represents the total of the wholesale prices of 96 different important commodities on the first day of each month—the average of the twelve months being taken as the average for the year.

Another method is to "weight" the prices of the various commodities as nearly as may be in proportion to the different quantities of them that enter into consumption. While there is no startling difference between the general movements of a weighted and an unweighted average, the preference should be given to the weighted average as more scientifically compiled, and that form is used in our graph of American commodity prices since 1850.

## METHOD OF INTERPRETATION

In general, the method of interpreting price movements must be historical. It is clear that the same causes would produce the same effects upon prices in the future as in the past. Exactly the same conditions will never be repeated, but the effect of each cause taken separately will nevertheless be the same.

Moreover, there is a striking similarity in the sets of conditions which are repeated at different times. The man whom in our childhood we were taught to call the wisest that ever lived, said that there is nothing new under the sun, and as regards principles his statement can still hardly be questioned. The aeroplane is new, but its principles date back to the later carboniferous period, when enormous bats and reptiles swarmed the air. The wireless is new, but only because we have just discovered the principle on which it is based. And the student of economic history, as he watches the interplay of forces which made the prices of the past, is much more surprised at the correspondences he discovers than at the differences.

Highly interesting, too, are the interrelations among the various graphs presented. We shall find that, within limits, each sheds light on all the others. And this fact is most important in enabling the observer to weave the whole into a well-informed and balanced view of the broad economic and financial situation.

The historical value of these statistics, also, should not be entirely ignored. To the reader who is of an observant and interpreting turn of mind, they give a better comprehension of the actual business conditions of the past than could be obtained by many hours of wading through the prosaic recitation of isolated facts and events. When we see, for example, the extraordinary and what would today be called prohibitive rates which the business man often had to pay for money in the '40s, '50s and '60s, we get a new and clearer comprehension of the industrial conditions of those times.

Among the influences which cause great and lasting changes we shall find that wars have an outstanding importance. This is because nothing else subverts conditions so widely or so radically. We have only to compare the Germany of today with the Germany of 1914 to see how far these changes may go; and although America has

## A CENTURY OF PRICES

not undergone any such vital or fundamental disorganization, yet she has experienced a transformation far greater than any other in her history except the Civil War. It is highly important to the banker, business man and investor to appreciate the character of that transformation and its bearing upon our future.

It is perhaps unnecessary to add that these chapters deal with broad tendencies and general principles. A minute examination of minor fluctuations and of the isolated historical events which caused them would be of little service to the business man, however interesting it might be to the student of history. We shall endeavor to dwell for the most part upon those factors which can be of practical help in the interpretation of the present and the future.

## CHAPTER II.

**GREAT ECONOMIC FORCES SINCE 1790**

IT is desirable first to view the operation of economic and financial forces in as broad a perspective as possible. In that way a better grasp of principles is obtained.

For this broad view the records of American conditions alone are inadequate. The United States before the Civil War was a new, detached, undeveloped nation. Its banking system was crude. Its supply of capital was trifling compared with its natural resources. Because of its great area, the imperfect means of communication and transportation then existing were entirely insufficient to weld it into an economic whole. And the business records of that time are fragmentary and incomplete.

England was the nation that, in the first half of the last century, had reached the highest industrial and financial development; and owing to her position as the world market for capital, a position which remained entirely secure until interfered with by the great war, her economic records are more representative of world business than any others available.

The two graphs showing the "Level of English Commodity Prices" since 1782 and the prices and yields of "British Consols" since 1790, reflect in condensed form English money market, investment and business conditions for a century and a quarter.

## COMMODITY PRICES

Taking up first the level of commodity prices, the primary fact must be recalled that a price represents not an absolute or

# A CENTURY OF PRICES

independent figure but a *relationship*—the relation of the value of the article priced to the value of gold or of whatever may be the standard money of the time.

Prices must therefore be viewed from two angles: The value of money on one side, and the value of goods or commodities on the other side. The idea of the money-value of goods is familiar; but its less familiar reciprocal, the goods-value of money, is equally significant.

Commodity prices, therefore may rise because commodities become worth more or because money becomes worth less; and they may fall because goods can be produced or manufactured more cheaply, or because money is growing scarcer in comparison with the work it has to do, and is therefore becoming more valuable because it is in relatively small supply.

Both these factors are in constant operation, sometimes the one being more important and sometimes the other. So the movements of the general level of commodity prices, like those of a sailboat crossing a river, are always the resultant of two forces acting at the same time.

Another influence of some importance as affecting the temporay and minor movements of commodity prices is what might be called "the psychology of prices." Buyers are more anxious to buy when other buyers are also anxious, and the same is true of sellers. So when a buying or selling movement is once well started it often carries prices beyond their natural level. Also, certain prices are so firmly established by custom that they are very slow to respond to actual changes in conditions. But these factors are of minor importance in considering the broad price movements of a century.

# A CENTURY OF PRICES

With these principles in mind, what are the economic and financial changes reflected by the movements of English commodity prices—which, it is to be remembered, broadly represent the prices of the whole commercial world?

The first point to strike the eye is the very great effect on prices of the Napoleonic Wars, 1793-1815, and the World War, 1914-1918. The highest price level of 1809 was more than 80 per cent. above that of 1789, the year of the French Revolution, and the English price level at the end of 1918 was approximately 125 per cent. above that of July, 1914. In each case (and also in our own Civil War, as will be seen later) high prices were due to a scarcity of products resulting from the great diversion of labor power into actual fighting forces and into war work and from the exceptional demands and wastes of war, together with

## A CENTURY OF PRICES

a big inflation of currency and credit.

No such tremendous advances in prices would be possible without more money, or more credit, or more of both. It takes twice as much money or credit to handle a thousand bushels of wheat at $2 a bushel, as at $1 a bushel, and the same with other commodities. If a greater supply of money or credit were not provided, the rise of prices resulting from scarcity of goods would soon cause "tight money," a condition which would seriously hamper and disturb the all-important war production.

In the late war both England and America endeavored to check the upward flight of prices by a policy of price-fixing. The results were not wholly satisfactory—notably in the cases of coal and wheat—but on the whole the experiment may perhaps be called a success as compared with what might have happened without such a policy. The only

## A CENTURY OF PRICES

policy which could entirely prevent rising prices in time of war would be a government control so complete as to amount to the theoretical socialistic state.

It will be noted that smaller wars, as the Crimean War and the American Civil War (comparatively small so far as the effects on the world at large were concerned), had a similar though less important effect on prices, and that a small price-boom followed the Franco-Prussian War.

In every case a decline from high war prices soon followed, but the extent and severity of the decline depended on numerous other conditions then entering the situation.

**EFFECT OF CHEAPER PRODUCTION**

The next point to be noted is that down to 1896 the broad tendency of prices had been downward for 87 years, although this tendency had been interrupted by numerous sharp rallies and by advances which, although of great significance at the time, eventually proved to have been temporary. If we take 1820 and 1900 as average years, not much affected by wars and representing neither the highest nor the lowest prices of those times, we note a decline from about 180 to 100, or about 45 per cent. of the higher figure.

The principal cause of this decline was the cheapening of production through improvements in machinery and in transportation. The machine-made shoe is cheaper than the hand-made shoe because less human labor is necessary to make it. Wheat raised by the aid of the tractor, the harvester and the threshing machine, and moved to market over the railroad, is cheaper than wheat sown and reaped by hand or by hand tools and hauled by horses over rough or muddy roads. And this transformation has

## A CENTURY OF PRICES

extended throughout all industry.

But why, it will be asked, in view of this continuously cheaper production, did prices rise from 1850 to 1873, nearly a quarter of a century, and from 1896 to 1914, when large-scale production was reaching its highest development? It is true that both 1850 and 1896 were periods of relative trade depression; but that fact alone does not answer the question. A more comprehensive reason must be sought.

The answer lies at the other end of the price-relationship—the supply of money. For although the supply of goods may be increasing, if the supply of money increases still faster, prices must soon rise.

In 1850 the worlds production of gold was approximately $40,000,000 annually. Through discoveries in California and in Australia, it rose to about $150,000,000 in 1853, fell to $91,000,000 in 1874, and did not again rise above the high point of the '50s until about 1893, when discoveries in the Klondyke and improved methods of mining resulted in another great increase, until $466,000,000 was reached in 1912. Since that date production has been comparatively stationary.

A better view, however, is obtained by considering the world's stock of gold on hand, since but little gold is consumed, in the ordinary sense of that word. This stock is estimated to have been about $2,200,000,000 in 1850; to have risen with reasonable regularity to about $6,000,000,000 in 1896, and thereafter at a more rapid rate to perhaps $11,000,000,000 in 1916.

In addition to this increase in the supply of gold, there has been a constant increase in the amount of credit based upon each dollar of gold, and credit serves the same purpose as money in the transaction of busi-

## A CENTURY OF PRICES

ness. In the United States, more than 95 per cent. of all payments are made by bank checks, which are a form of credit.

We conclude, therefore, that from 1850 to 1873 the increase in the supply of money and credit was, broadly speaking, more rapid than the increase in the supply of commodities through cheaper methods of production, so that prices rose (aided somewhat by three wars); that from 1873 to 1896 the increased production of commodities got the upper hand, causing a general decline in prices; while after 1896 a further great increase in gold production and in the use of instruments of credit turned the scale and brought higher commodity prices.

The reasons for many of the minor changes in the level of prices are shown upon the graph. It is noticeable that these minor changes have become less violent

# A CENTURY OF PRICES

with the passage of time, a highly desirable development. If some plan could be invented to keep the general level of commodity prices stationary it would be an almost inestimable boon, but apparently such a plan would have to be world-wide in its application. Several ingenious methods have been suggested, but they seem to require a much higher plane of world-organization than has yet been attained.

## THE SUPPLY OF CAPITAL

The best index to the relative supply of capital over such a long period as is here considered, is to be found in the yield on the British consolidated debt. Consols have no date of maturity and have a longer continuous record than any other security. Both prices and yields (the latter inverted) are shown on the graph for completeness, as the rate of interest has twice been reduced.

# A CENTURY OF PRICES

There are, of course, two main elements in these prices—the credit of the British nation, and the relation between the demand and supply of capital for investment. From 1816 to 1914 British credit stood so high that changes in the yield on consols were due almost entirely to variations in the demand and supply of capital; but the Napoleonic Wars and the World War of 1914 caused such a vast increase in the British debt that national credit was somewhat affected, and consols fell for that reason as well as because of the rapid dissipation of capital in war. But there can be no question that the main cause of changes in the price of consols lies in the relative supply of capital in comparison with demand.

We have already noted that the broad downward trend in commodity prices until 1896 was due chiefly to the increase in the productive capacity of labor through im-

## A CENTURY OF PRICES

provements in machinery and in transportation. The same influence caused an increase in the supply of capital compared with the demand for it which was reflected in rising prices for consols from 1798 until 1896. In fact, after 1825, by which date British credit was thoroughly re-established, the accumulation of capital in excess of current needs was the principal cause of the rise in consols.

This, among other considerations, led to a pretty general belief, in the late '90s, that the interest rate on capital would continue to fall, or at any rate would not rise materially. The reasoning seemed clear: Improved methods of applying labor caused greater production of wealth, which in turn resulted in greater proportional accumulation of capital. This had caused rising bond prices and falling income yields for nearly a century. The presumption was exceedingly strong that the same causes would continue to operate and to produce a similar effect.

The same causes did continue to operate; but as we have seen in discussing commodity prices, another very powerful influence counteracted and overbalanced them from about 1896 onward—the fact that the supply of money and credit was increasing even more rapidly than the supply of goods, and thus forcing commodity prices upward.

**THE FLOW OF CAPITAL**

At first thought it would seem that easier money and credit should cause higher prices for consols and other similar securities. Temporarily, they do have that effect, because of the accumulation of deposits—or *liquid* capital—in the banks. This liquid capital immediately tends to flow into securities and therefore raises their prices. But this is a temporary effect only. Liquid capital very soon flows *through* securities, and by means of government, municipal, or corporate expenditures, into concrete and tangible things. In fact, the securities are issued only for the purpose of securing capital for expenditure upon these concrete and tangible things.

The capital which flows into consols, for example, is not held idle by the British Government. It is soon *spent,* for one purpose or another, and the spending means the employment of labor, the purchase of materials and supplies—in short, the prompt turning of liquid capital into tangible property. Let us suppose that consols are sold in order to erect a big government building. Then the capital which is absorbed into the consols is immediately converted into marble, bricks, structural steel, food, clothing and supplies for workmen, etc. And this is true of the capital which is invested in any and all securities.

## A CENTURY OF PRICES

Thus the offset of increased gold production and enlargement of credit facilities, although *first felt* in the money and credit markets, immediately passes *through* them and finds its more permanent manifestation in rising commodity prices.

*Bond yields must rise (and bond prices fall) with any prolonged advance in commodity prices.* The bond investor, through long habit, thinks of his interest return in terms of money; but when he starts to make use of that interest return, what it will buy for him depends upon the level of commodity prices. If commodity prices rise while his interest return remains stationary, he soon finds that his *real* income has shrunk. His money income must rise with advancing commodity prices, for exactly the same reason that the wages of labor must rise.

It is equally true that rising commodity prices reduce the supply of investment capi-

## A CENTURY OF PRICES

tal and thus raise its price—that is, the rate of interest return on securities. We have just seen that capital, as it accumulates, flows quickly through securities and into commodities; so when the prices of those commodities rise, they necessarily absorb more capital. In the example just mentioned above, if the prices of building materials and labor double, it will take twice as much capital to construct the government building.

The connection between bond yields, or the price of investment capital, and the level of commodity prices is therefore very much closer than has been generally appreciated. And this is even more evident from the record of history, as shown in these graphs, than it from *a priori* reasoning.

In comparing the two graphs, we see at once that the graph of consols is, in a broad way, the reverse of the graph of commodity prices. Even in the irregularities of the Napoleonic Wars, which are only partly comparable with modern conditions, low consols and high commodities roughly coincided, and from about 1805 to 1896 the reverse correspondence is very plain. But the clearest demonstration of the principle is seen from 1896 to date, when a sudden turn in commodity prices was followed within two years by an equally sharp change in consols, with an almost perfect reverse correspondence in the two price-lines down to the present time.

**POST-WAR PRICE MOVEMENTS**

It will be seen from these graphs that every war which had a direct and important effect upon business conditions in England was preceded or accompanied by a rise in commodity prices and a fall in consols, and that *after* every such war (except the Boer

## "A CENTURY OF PRICES"

War) commodity prices fell and consols rose. Even following the Boer War the long upward movement of commodity prices then in progres was checked for half a dozen years, and the yield on consols for some years showed a reactionary tendency, though without any highly significant change.

Later graphs will show us that the same tendencies were strongly evident in the United States during and after the Civil War.

We are fairly safe, then, in concluding that this is a law of post-war price movements, which may be modified, but rarely, if ever, nullified, by other influences, and that there is now a very strong probability of a gradually declining tendency in English commodity prices and a rising tendency in consols and similar securities for some years to come.

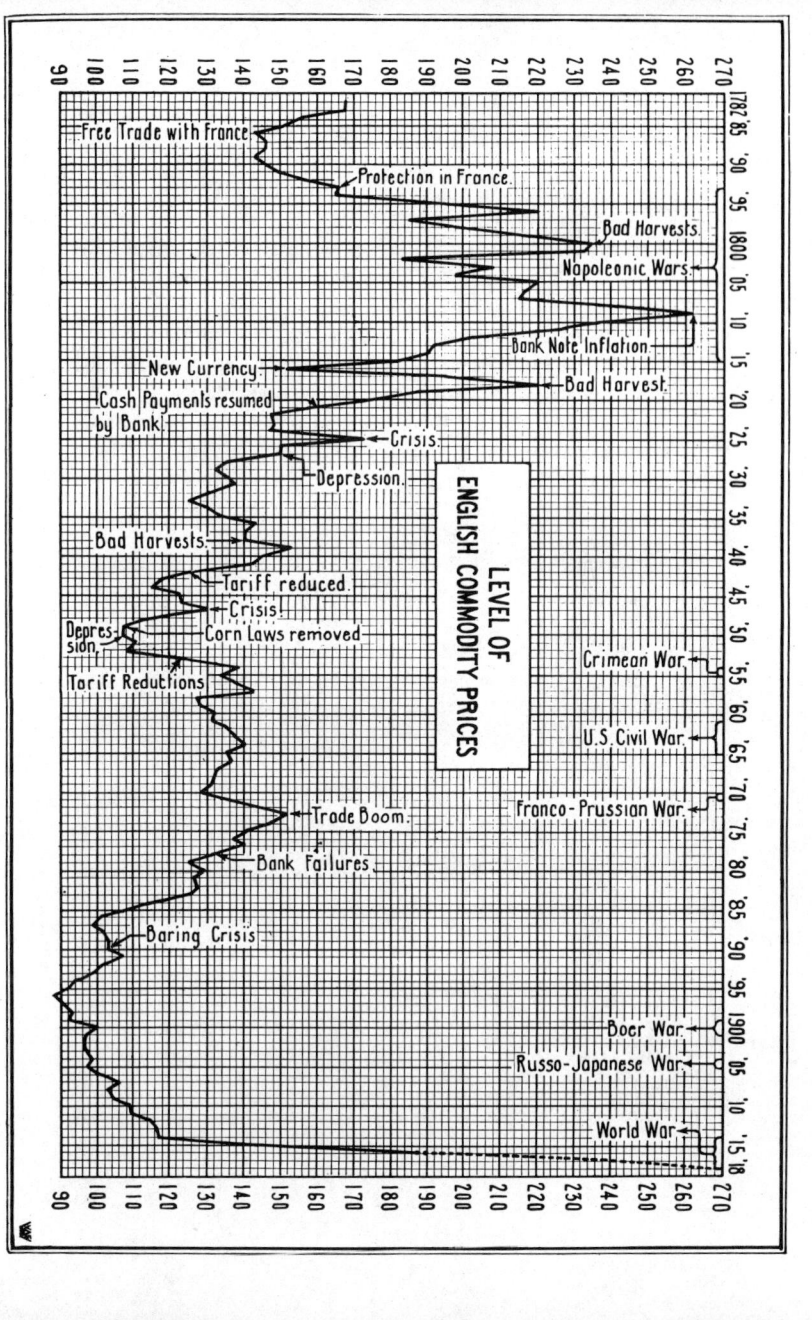

# LEVEL OF ENGLISH COMMODITY PRICES

- Free Trade with France
- Protection in France
- Bad Harvests
- Napoleonic Wars
- Bank Note Inflation
- New Currency
- Bad Harvest
- Cash Payments resumed by Bank
- Crisis
- Depression
- Bad Harvests
- Tariff reduced
- Crisis
- Corn Laws removed
- Depression
- Tariff Reductions
- Crimean War
- U.S. Civil War
- Franco-Prussian War
- Trade Boom
- Bank Failures
- Baring Crisis
- Boer War
- Russo-Japanese War
- World War

# NOTATIONS TO CHARTS
## ON PAGES 43 AND 45

### Level of English Commodity Prices

This continuous index of English commodity prices since 1782 is (with the exception of the last two years) from *Todd's Mechanism of Exchange*. It is based on Jevon's index down to 1860, Sauerbeck's 1860-70, the British Board of Trade index 1871-1916, and the *Economist* number for 1917 and 1918, the first, third and fourth having been recalculated to fit the third. These substitutions do not seriously affect the value of the line as a continuous record.

### British Consols

British Consols afford the longest continuous security record obtainable. They have no date of maturity. The interest rate was 3% down to 1888, 2¾% from 1889 to 1903, 2½% from 1904 to date. Since the change in the rate affected the price, we show also the yield throughout the period, the scale being reversed to make the line comparable with the prices.

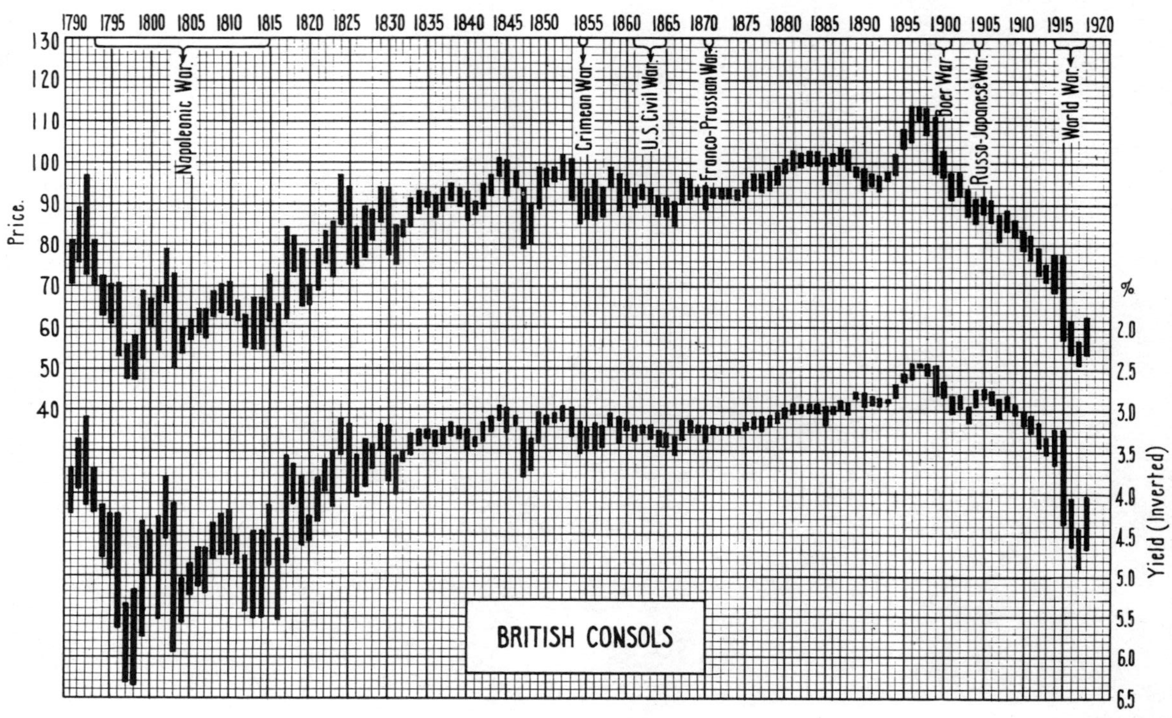
BRITISH CONSOLS
Price.
Yield (Inverted)
%
1790 1795 1800 1805 1810 1815 1820 1825 1830 1835 1840 1845 1850 1855 1860 1865 1870 1875 1880 1885 1890 1895 1900 1905 1910 1915 1920
130 120 110 100 90 80 70 60 50 40
2.0 2.5 3.0 3.5 4.0 4.5 5.0 5.5 6.0 6.5
Napoleonic War.
Crimean War.
U.S. Civil War.
Franco-Prussian War.
Boer War.
Russo-Japanese War.
World War.

## CHAPTER III.

### WHAT AMERICAN COMMODITY PRICES SHOW

AS would naturally be expected, the broad principles affecting the movements of American commodity prices have been the same as those brought out in connection with English prices in the last chapter.

In America as in Europe, great wars have caused rapid advances in prices; after those wars prices have fallen, though not so rapidly as they had previously risen. From 1865 to 1897 the prolonged decline was in large part due to the effect of machinery and improved transportation in cheapening production; increased gold production

## A CENTURY OF PRICES

played an important part in the rise of prices preceding the Civil War and following 1897; the influence of speculation in "boom" periods is plainly visible; and the expansion of currency and credit has had its due effect.

On the other hand, there are marked differences in the degree to which these several factors have entered the situation at different times.

It is impracticable to compile any trustworthy average of American commodity prices previous to 1850. Falkner's Index, it is true, runs back to 1840, but owing to the numerous interpolations and changes necessary in the earlier years it has obvious defects. Since 1850 commodity prices as shown in the accompanying graph afford a reasonably accurate view of the broad trend of prices. During and following the Civil War prices in currency are shown by the

# A CENTURY OF PRICES

dotted line, while the continuous line shows prices in gold, then selling at a considerable premium in currency.

## CAUSES OF WAR PRICES

In this way we get a fairly accurate measure of the effect of currency inflation in the Civil War, but it is impossible to make any similar comparison during the World War, from 1914 to 1918. Up to 1917, when the United States entered the war, the increase in our currency was nearly all in gold—"gold inflation," it has been called—because our big sales of war supplies to Europe brought a flood of the yellow metal to our shores. In 1917 and 1918 the currency increase was in the form of Federal reserve notes, the result of rediscounting of Government and commercial paper at the Federal banks, rendered possible through the great change which had been made in our banking system.

## A CENTURY OF PRICES

There was, therefore, an increase in the volume of our currency and credit which, in its practical effects, amounted to inflation; but there was no premium on gold by which to measure the degree of inflation as in the Civil War. And of course another important difference lies in the fact that the present currency inflation, in one form or another, is almost world-wide, while in the Civil War it was confined to the United States.

We see at once, however, that the high Civil War prices were by no means entirely due to the depreciation of the currency. From 1863 to 1866 our prices in gold rose about 47 per cent., although English prices were nearly stationary in those years. This advance compares with a rise of about 87 per cent in American prices from 1914 to 1918—and as we have just seen, the latter advance was accompanied by a great in-

## A CENTURY OF PRICES

crease in outstanding currency, while during the Civil War gold was hoarded to such an extent that only about $25,000,000 is estimated by the director of the United States Mint to have been in circulation after 1861.

Comparing English and American (gold) prices from 1849, the year of the California gold discoveries, to 1873, which was the highest point of English prices between 1840 and 1915, we find that the rise in each country was almost exactly 83 per cent. But from 1864 to 1872 American (gold) prices were relatively higher than those of England—from 1865 to 1867, much higher. This fact must be attributed almost entirely to scarcity of goods resulting from diversion of labor and materials into the war and from special war demands and war wastes.

The great rise in Civil War prices as expressed in *currency*—the dotted line on the graph—was due partly to the increase in

# A CENTURY OF PRICES

the volume of currency and partly to actual distrust of the Government's ability to redeem its notes. Even though the Civil War greenbacks had been immediately redeemable in gold, there must have been, if the same quantity of them had been issued, a great rise in prices; but in addition to this inevitable rise, a further advance occurred because the relatively insecure financial position of the United States Government at that time lowered the value of its notes.

During the World War this element of doubt as to the United States Government's credit did not exist. Therefore the advance of American prices from 1914 to 1918 was due almost entirely to the war demand, which was permitted to express itself in prices through currency and credit expansion and the increase in our stocks of gold.

The war prices of 1918 reached substantially the same level as the *currency* prices of 1865; but it would be entirely unsafe to assume that prices will fall from that high level as rapidly as they did in 1866 and following years.

Two very important differences must be borne in mind: (1) The currency prices of 1865 were made in a *depreciated* money —depreciated as compared with gold. That was not true in 1918. Our currency was then greatly expanded, by imports of gold and by the issue of Federal reserve notes; our outstanding bank credits were tremendously enlarged; but the element of depreciation as compared with gold did not enter the situation at all.

(2) In 1865 our price level, as expressed in our currency, was enormously above the price levels of the rest of the world. Even our gold prices, as we have seen, were relatively higher than those of England. But

our 1918 prices were relatively *lower* than those of Europe. English prices of 1918 were approximately 130 per cent above those of 1914, while our 1918 prices were about 88 per cent higher than 1914.

After the Civil War our prices returned to their pre-war level but, for the reasons above outlined, that is not likely to happen after the present war. The world has learned to make its supply of gold safely support a larger amount of currency and credit and the change will be to some extent permanent. Therefore a higher level of commodity prices is likely to be maintained, though not the extreme level created by the pinch of war.

## COMMODITY PRICES AND OUR EXPORT TRADE

In comparing the graph of American commodity prices with that of English prices shown in Chapter II, we see that there is a fairly close correspondence be-

# A CENTURY OF PRICES

tween the two, and that it tends to become closer with the passage of time.

This is not only because the same principles necessarily apply to both, but also because quicker and cheaper communication between America and Europe leads, over a long period of years, to a readier exchange of goods.

Whenever our price level rises above that of other nations we become a relatively good market in which to sell goods and a poor market in which to buy, so that our imports increase and our exports decrease, and when our price level falls to a relatively low plane this condition is reversed. But increased exports soon bring imports of gold to pay for them, and the addition of this gold to our supply of currency tends to raise our price level. In the same way increased imports cause us to send gold abroad to pay for the goods received, thus reducing the gold base of our currency and credit and tending to reduce our price level to the point where foreigners cannot get so great a profit by shipping us their goods, and therefore our imports fall off.

In this way our exports and imports of merchandise constantly tend to adjust our price level to the level which prevails in other countries. Prices throughout the commercial world are a question of international adjustment through exchange of goods and gold.

There is, however, a constant margin between what might be called the export level and the import level. Foreigners will not sell us goods until our prices are enough higher than theirs to cover the cost of placing the goods in our hands, and we will not sell them goods unless our domestic prices are enough lower than theirs so that we can afford to stand the cost of shipping

## A CENTURY OF PRICES

the goods to them. Between these two price levels there must always be a margin, depending on the cost of transportation, tariffs, and the rates of foreign exchange.

The question of the relation between American and foreign price-levels and its effect upon our exports, and through them upon our domestic business also, is one of much interest. Our "export balance" from year to year reflects very clearly not only this price-relationship but also the progress of the "major trade cycle," as it is called—the broad swing of business activity from prosperity to depression and back again, covering a period of something like twenty years, which has been such a noticeable feature of our trade since 1837.

The small graph herewith, showing the per cent of our export balance yearly to our total foreign trade, in comparison with the ratio of English to American commodity

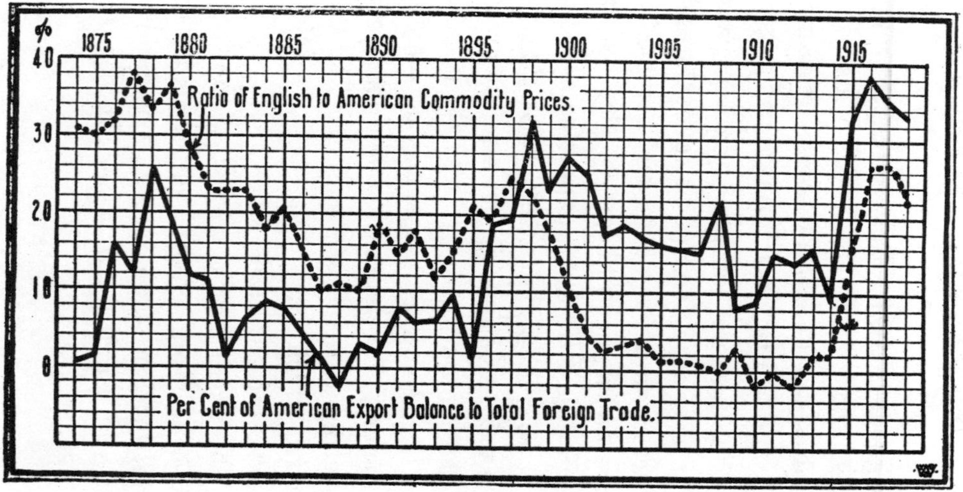
%
40
30
20
10
0
1875
1880
1885
1890
1895
1900
1905
1910
1915
Ratio of English to American Commodity Prices.
Per Cent of American Export Balance to Total Foreign Trade.

## A CENTURY OF PRICES

prices, makes these relationships quickly intelligible to the eye.*

As would naturally be expected, the largest exports have usually occurred at times when English prices were relatively high compared with ours. The correspondence would be still closer but for the fact that during the most of this period our exports consisted almost entirely of agricultural products and were therefore dependent upon crop conditions as well as upon prices.

---

*The export balance is shown in this form rather than in dollars in order to eliminate the change due to the rapid growth of our trade, thus affording a line which is fairly comparable one year with another throughout the entire period. No scale is shown for the line giving the ratio of English to American prices, since it expresses merely a relationship and the figures themselves have no significance. This line is obtained by dividing the English index numbers by the American index numbers. The fact that English prices were lower, compared with those of America, from 1902 to 1914, than they were from 1882 to 1894, was chiefly due to the great reduction in transportation costs between the two countries.

## A CENTURY OF PRICES

Those who are familiar with the business history of the United States will immediately note, on looking over this graph, that the high points of our export trade were in each instance followed by great prosperity, while small exports have, broadly speaking, accompanied periods of relatively poor general business. The principal reason why a large balance of exports over imports has such an emphatically stimulating effect upon our trade as a whole is because it results in an inflow of gold from foreign countries. Our chief use for gold is in bank reserves, where it permits an expansion of credit formerly equal to about five times the amount of the gold and, under our new Federal bank law, to a good deal more than that ratio. Easy credit is the life of trade; hence the pronounced effect of gold imports.

Down to 1877 we regularly imported

## A CENTURY OF PRICES

more merchandise than we exported and sent gold abroad to pay for it—being a gold-producing nation. But between 1872 and 1878 a great change occurred. Our imports of merchandise gradually fell from $656,000,000 to $432,000,000, while at the same time our exports increased from $469,000,000 to $737,000,000. The result is shown in the sharp rise of the "export balance" line on the graph. Large gold imports followed. From 1870 to 1875 our average excess of gold exports was about $36,500,000; but from 1879 to 1881 our average excess of gold imports was $66,700,000 yearly. It was this gold in our bank reserves which permitted the rapid business expansion of that period.

Similar conditions followed the great increase in our exports of merchandise which began in 1896, and again the great movement of 1915 and following years.

# A CENTURY OF PRICES

## THE MAJOR CYCLE

The small graph also defines clearly the swing of the "major cycle" of prosperity and depression. Without attempting to go deeply into fundamental causes, we may note that the year 1916 in the current cycle appears to correspond closely to the years 1898 and 1878 in the two preceding cycles, after which in each case generally prosperous business conditions prevailed for some years.

Moreover, we cannot leave out of our calculations in this connection the very large payments due this country from Europe for interest and principal of indebtedness incurred during the last few years. It is a question just how these payments are to be met. But in any case they must certainly tend to increase our national income as compared with the years before the war.

The graph showing wheat and cotton

## A CENTURY OF PRICES

prices is less suggestive of general principles than that covering the average of all commodities. The two important factors which cause abnormally high prices for wheat in certain years are wars and crop scarcity. Their effect is plainly shown and the reasons for it are self-evident in view of what has been said in regard to the movements of commodity prices in general.

The famine prices for cotton in the Civil War were due to the blockade of Southern ports—practically no cotton being raised anywhere else in the world at that date. Since cotton is easily stored and can be carried over from year to year, speculation has in recent years become a notable factor in its price. Producers have made strong efforts, by storing their cotton and by reducing the acreage devoted to it, to maintain prices at a good level. Since fixed prices were not applied to cotton in the

## A CENTURY OF PRICES

World War, it reflected fully the speculative spirit and the exceptional demands of the time.

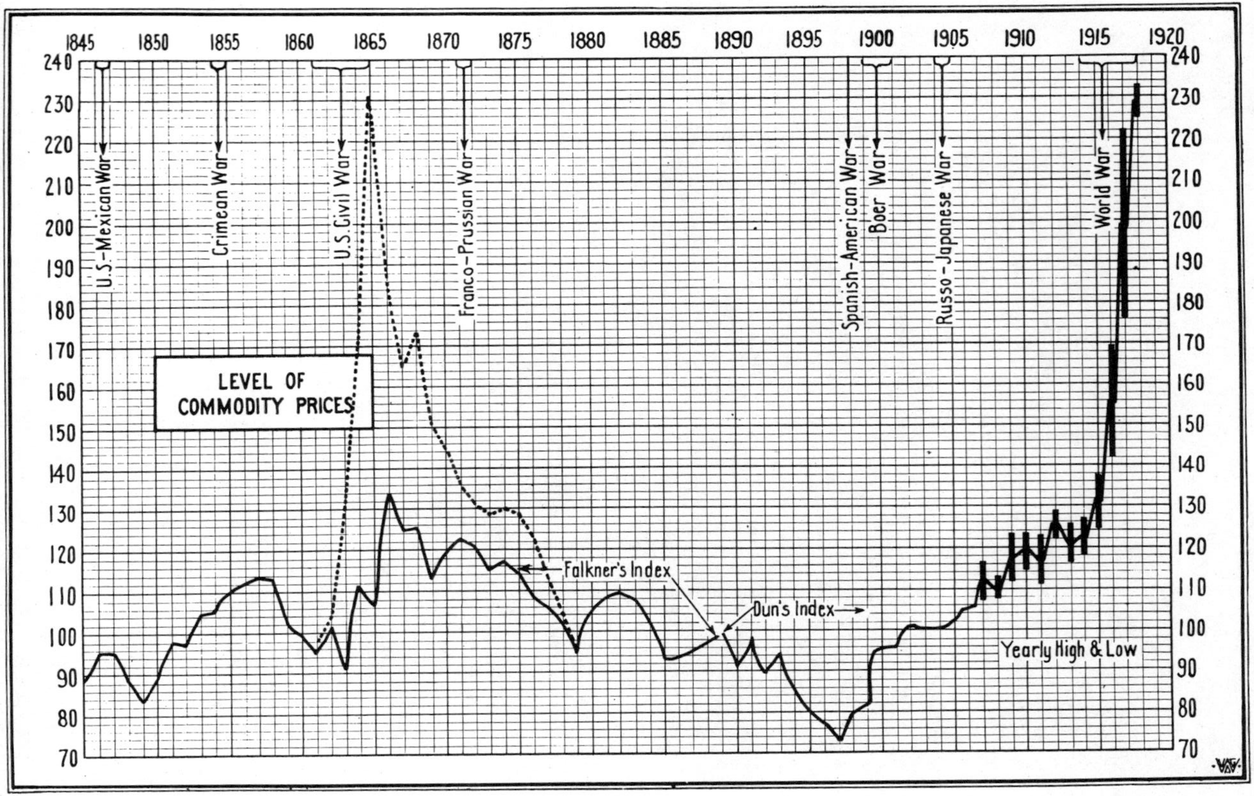
LEVEL OF
COMMODITY PRICES
U.S.-Mexican War
Crimean War
U.S. Civil War
Franco-Prussian War
Spanish-American War
Boer War
Russo-Japanese War
World War
Falkner's Index
Dun's Index
Yearly High & Low
1845
1850
1855
1860
1865
1870
1875
1880
1885
1890
1895
1900
1905
1910
1915
1920
70
80
90
100
110
120
130
140
150
160
170
180
190
200
210
220
230
240

# NOTATIONS TO CHARTS
# ON PAGES 65 AND 67

## Level of Commodity Prices

The weighted form of Falkner's index of commodity prices, as prepared for the Aldrich Report on Wholesale Prices to the United States Senate, is here used down to 1889. Down to 1850 the figures upon which it was based were somewhat fragmentary. In 1889 Dun's and Falkner's indices were practically the same, and from that point to date Dun's is used. It is a weighted average of wholesale prices of all important commodities. The various indices compiled by different authorities show only minor variations in the general trend. During and after the Civil War the dotted line shows prices in the depreciated currency of the period, and the continuous line shows the equivalent in gold. The gold prices are not strictly comparable with prices before and after this period. The prices of many articles continued to be fixed by custom, so that the full effect of the gold premium was not felt.

## Wheat—No. 2 at Chicago and
## Cash Cotton at New York

There has been a continuous market for cash cotton at New York since 1820, but for wheat the prices before the Civil War varied greatly in different parts of the country and there was no such system of standard grades as came into use later. After the completion of the Erie Canal, Albany occupied about the same relative position in the trade as Chicago occupies now, but the price records of that time were unfortunately destroyed by fire at the State Capitol a few years ago.

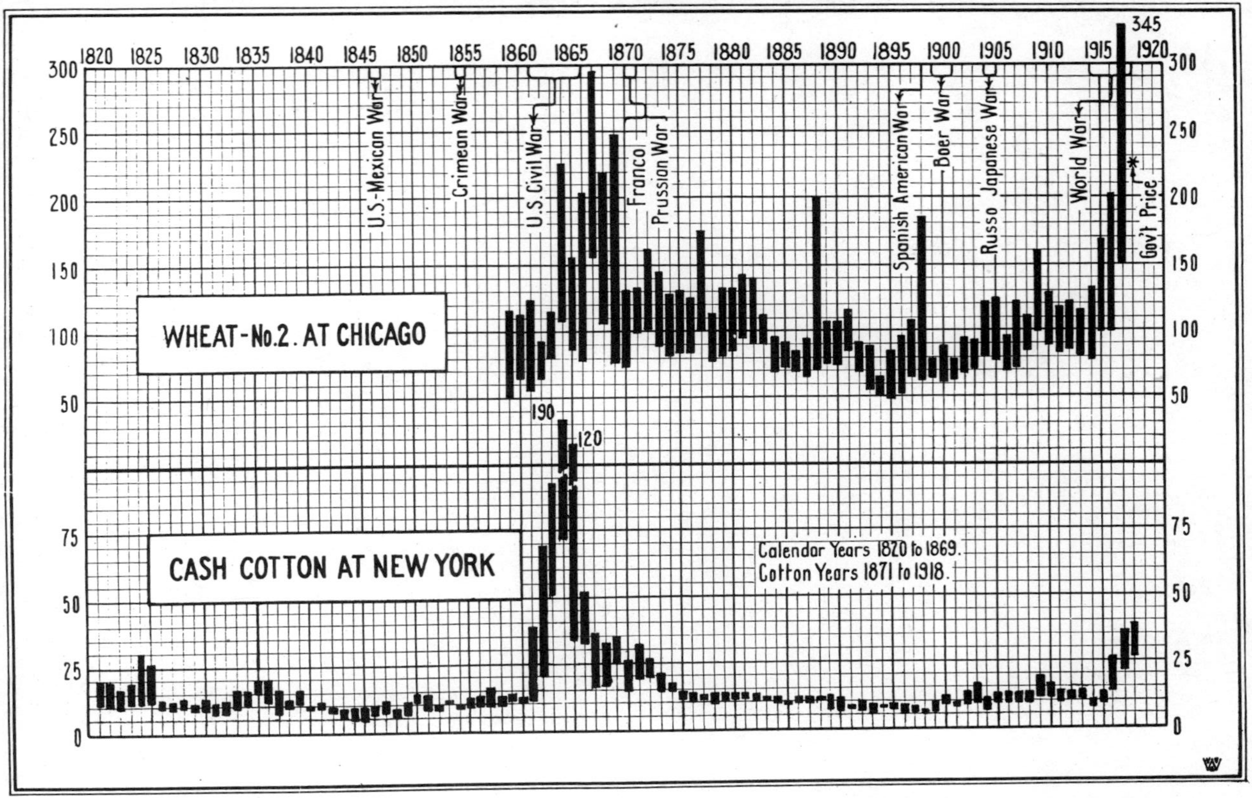

WHEAT-No.2. AT CHICAGO
CASH COTTON AT NEW YORK
U.S.-Mexican War
Crimean War
U.S. Civil War
Franco Prussion War
Spanish American War
Boer War
Russo Japanese War
World War
Gov't Price
345
190
120
Calendar Years 1820 to 1869.
Cotton Years 1871 to 1918.
1820 1825 1830 1835 1840 1845 1850 1855 1860 1865 1870 1875 1880 1885 1890 1895 1900 1905 1910 1915 1920
300 250 200 150 100 50
75 50 25 0

## CHAPTER IV.

## CAUSES OF CHANGES IN INTEREST YIELDS AND MONEY RATES

THE fact is obvious that the average investment yield obtainable from bonds or loans must depend on the supply of capital as compared with the demand for it. It is essential, therefore, in considering the changes shown on the graphs of bond yields and money rates, to examine the conditions affecting capital during the period covered.

"When people talk to me about money and capital," complained a member of the Stock Exchange, "I begin to get a headache." To avoid such headaches it is necessary to understand thoroughly what capital is, a point in regard to which even bankers of long experience are often hazy.

# A CENTURY OF PRICES

To begin at the beginning, all capital is the product of labor. It is labor-product saved, set aside and stored up to aid in further production, instead of being used up in current consumption. A farmer, for example, can spend his year's surplus income for a new piano, which is not capital unless it can be shown that it will increase the total production of the farm; or he may spend his surplus on a tractor, which is capital because it will increase his product. And if he lends his year's surplus to a neighbor, or turns it over to a bank, or invests it in a bond, he is entitled to interest, because in that case he is denying himself both the piano and the tractor.

**FACTORS IN THE SUPPLY OF CAPITAL**

The supply of capital available at any time, therefore, will depend on a number of considerations:—

(1) The total amount of labor applied.

## A CENTURY OF PRICES

To accumulate capital a nation must be industrious. A sluggish, unambitious population merely earns its living as it goes along, without piling up any surplus.

(2) The efficiency of labor—the amount of the product in comparison with the labor applied. This depends chiefly upon the extent to which machinery is employed, but also upon the energy and faithfulness of the workmen.

(3) What is being done with the labor-product; whether it is:

(*a*) Being used up for current consumption—for food, clothing, luxuries, pleasure trips, etc.

(*b*) Being invested in tools, equipment, and improvements which will bring an immediate return in the form of increased production.

(*c*) Going into improvements of a more permanent character, which will be of public or private benefit eventually, but will not yield any early returns in the form of greater production.

The third consideration above mentioned brings up another very important point, namely, the rapidity with which capital circulates when used in different ways. For very little capital is permanently fixed in one form.

The tractor wears itself out in creating an increased product of other things; its value is gradually transferred into those other things; the capital invested in it *circulates*. The factory depreciates. The railroad's rails, ties and roadbed have to be constantly renewed. Its stations have to be repaired frequently and finally become antiquated and have to be rebuilt.

Even the Roman viaducts, perhaps the most permanent investment of capital in history, eventually fall into disrepair. The

## A CENTURY OF PRICES

original investment in the Suez Canal, or in New York's water works, might perhaps be mentioned as permanently fixed, although additional expenditures are constantly necessary for maintenance and betterments.

So the extent to which any particular use of capital depletes the general supply depends not only on the amount of capital used but also on *how long it is used*. The farm tractor may, by increasing the farmer's product, reproduce its value in a year. A new barn might not pay for itself, through increased production due to better facilities, in less than twenty years. Even if the first cost of the two were the same, the barn would eventually require twenty times as much use of capital as the tractor.

Capital may be roughly classified according to the rapidity with which it circulates, as follows:—

# A CENTURY OF PRICES

(1) Capital in the form of commodities. Some of these are luxuries, but most of them contribute toward further production and are therefore capital. In this form capital circulates rapidly.

(2) Capital invested in machinery or equipment, or in enterprises which will be immediately productive, circulates less rapidly, as a rule, than commodities, but more rapidly than in the forms mentioned below.

(3) Investments in enterprises which will eventually yield a return, but only after considerable delay.

(4) Expenditures for public benefit, such as court houses, schools, playgrounds, baths, etc. These contribute indirectly to the future productive capacity of the people.

(5) Investments in enterprises which fail, or expenditures in war. This capital stops circulating. In some cases a small part

of it may, however, be salvaged.

An increased application of capital to any one of these five divisions will necessarily tend to deplete the current supply of capital, and therefore to bring higher interest yields; but the effect in this direction will be far greater and more permanent if the capital goes into relatively fixed forms, or into forms where its circulation is slow, than it will be when the capital is applied where it will circulate rapidly.

Hence the great importance of distinguishing between *fixed* and *circulating* capital.

**RISE AND FALL OF BOND YIELDS**

In Chapter II, in discussing the relation between the level of English commodity prices and the yield on consols, we noted the close correspondence in the general trend of the two. In comparing the graph of U. S. Corporation Bond Yields with that

## A CENTURY OF PRICES

of American Commodity Prices (discussed in Chapter III), we find the same broad correspondence.

We are now in a position, after refreshing our memory as to the nature of capital, to define more accurately the reasons for this correspondence. The superficial reason why bond yields rise with rising commodity prices is that the investor, finding his *real* income shrinking although his money income is unchanged, demands a higher rate of interest, but he would not be able to obtain this higher rate if it were not for the fact the supply of capital is smaller in comparison with the demand for it. And the reason why higher commodity prices so greatly increase the demand for capital is that *they bring a nearly proportional increase in the cost of capital investments in all of the five divisions above enumerated.*

The capital which, at any one time, exists

in the form of commodities, is only a small part of the total capital of the country and circulates rapidly. Therefore a rise in the prices of commodities would have only a moderate effect toward increasing the demand for capital. But all investments of capital (usually after passing through the form of securities, as previously explained) are first expended on materials and labor —that is, on commodities and on wages, which roughly follow changes in the price-level of commodities, though usually lagging behind somewhat.

If, for example, the price-level of commodities has risen 50 per cent, the cost of a new courthouse, or a new railroad, or a mine, or a subway system, will also be found to have risen nearly 50 per cent; so that the amount of capital required for investment in relatively fixed forms rises in rough proportion with the rise in commodity prices. It is this increase in the cost of fixed forms of investment which rapidly depletes the supply of investment capital and therefore raises its price, which is best expressed in the form of the average yield on bonds.

During a period of falling commodity prices the situation is, of course, exactly reversed, so that bond yields tend to follow commodity prices downward.

**DIVERSION OF CAPITAL INTO FIXED FORMS**

Another important element affecting the demand and supply of capital is the *relative extent* to which capital is diverted into fixed forms, especially those expenditures which contemplate a somewhat remote public benefit; or into investments in enterprises which prove failures, or the cost of wars.

The Panama Canal, the New York State

barge canal, the New York City subway system, are examples of undertakings that have absorbed great quantities of capital from which only a trifling immediate return can be expected. Municipal and State expenditures for varied improvements have increased rapidly in recent years, and however desirable such investments may be with a view to the longer future, immediate cash returns from them are apt to be small.

And added to these factors came the tremendous depletion of the whole world's capital in the war.

It is a question, also, whether the people's disposition to save has not grown less within the last two decades—whether the average man does not now save a smaller percentage of his income than he saved in the first years of the twentieth century. If so, this tends to cut off the supply of capital at its source.

## A CENTURY OF PRICES

These several influences tend to act in harmony. Rising commodity prices increase profits—as measured in money—and infuse the public in general with a spirit of liberality in expenditure, so that costly improvements are more readily undertaken, living expenses grow at the expense of savings, and the people are more prone to invest in doubtful speculations or fake stocks. In time of war, also, great expenditures of capital coincide with a rapid rise in commodity prices.

The great fall in bond yields from the period of the '70s to 1900 was partly due to the better standing and stronger protection of our corporation bonds as a whole in the later years; but it was also largely due to the great increase in production of goods as a result of improvements in machinery and transportation. When labor produces more goods it is naturally easier to accumulate capital.

# A CENTURY OF PRICES

### MONEY RATES

Money rates and bond yields mutually influence each other, since both represent the return on the use of capital; but since the term "money rates" is applied only to loans for short periods, changes in these rates are chiefly dependent upon temporary conditions, while changes in bond yields are chiefly dependent upon conditions of a more permanent character.

A comparison of the two graphs shows that sharp changes in money rates are sympathetically reflected in the *minor movements* of bond yields, but that money rates have very little to do with the broad sweep of the bond market.

Rates on call money and 30 or 60-day loans have in the past fluctuated so quickly as a result of temporary conditions that they are of little value for comparison over long periods. Commercial paper affords the true that commercial paper affords the broadest and best index to general money conditions.

Unusually high money rates and the minor and temporary upward swings in bond yields are commonly due to an overextended condition of bank loans—that is, a scarcity of credit accommodation. Scarcity of credit means that borrowers must pay a higher price for it, so money rates rise. And if a higher rate of interest is obtainable from short loans than from bonds, capital is temporarily attracted away from the bond market, and owners of bonds are tempted to switch into commercial paper or time loans, so that bond prices fall and yields rise.

This condition of overextended bank loans may be due to too great optimism in business circles, which leads business men to branch out too widely and too rapidly,

## A CENTURY OF PRICES

and thus to use up an undue proportion of the credit available; or it may be due to events which arouse a widespread feeling of fear as to the future, so that there is a general desire to call in loans and contract credits. Before long the first condition is very apt to precipitate the second, but the second does not necessarily imply the first.

Thus in 1857, 1873, 1893 and 1907 the primary cause of high rates was overexpansion. But in 1861 fear was aroused by the beginning of the Civil War; in 1890 by the Baring failure; in 1896 by danger to the gold standard; in 1914 by the outbreak of the World War; and in none of these cases was any special overexpansion in evidence.

The high money rates reached in most of the years previous to 1874 reflect in a very interesting way the scarcity of credit and liquid capital in those times. The high figures were usually reached in the fall,

## A CENTURY OF PRICES

when the crops were being moved. Conditions of doing business when an average rate of 10 per cent must be paid for money are entirely different from those when the average rate is 5 per cent. Before and during the Civil War any firm had to earn large profits in order to stay in business, and the constant wide fluctuations in rates introduced an element of uncertainty now happily absent.

The extreme high rates of panic years, as in 1857, 1861 and 1873, simply mean that during the panic periods money was practically unobtainable. Failures were so numerous that even the highest class two-name commercial paper was subject to suspicion. Yet that suspicion was not the chief cause of the high rates. The real reason was the absolute lack of loanable funds.

We have today very little conception of conditions such as those of the panic of

## A CENTURY OF PRICES

1857, for example. The newspapers at that time reported that in some instances 2½ per cent a day was bid for call loans. Leading banks and old, conservative business houses were falling right and left like ninepins. For loans of four to six months on prime commercial paper 3 per cent a month was offered, and doubtless higher rates would have been paid if there had been a prospect of bringing out the money. One of the market reports stated that the money market was in a state of "anarchy." Gold commanded 8 per cent premium at Baltimore, and the general disorganization of business was far beyond anything known to the present generation.

Under the improved banking methods now in use it is to be expected that fluctuations in money rates will be much narrower than in even the recent past. Commercial paper rates during the war were successfully stabilized at or below 6 per cent, and while it is possible that periods of rapid expansion may sometimes carry them temporarily over that figure, it is highly probable that extremely high rates for time money and commercial paper will no longer be a recurrent feature of the markets.

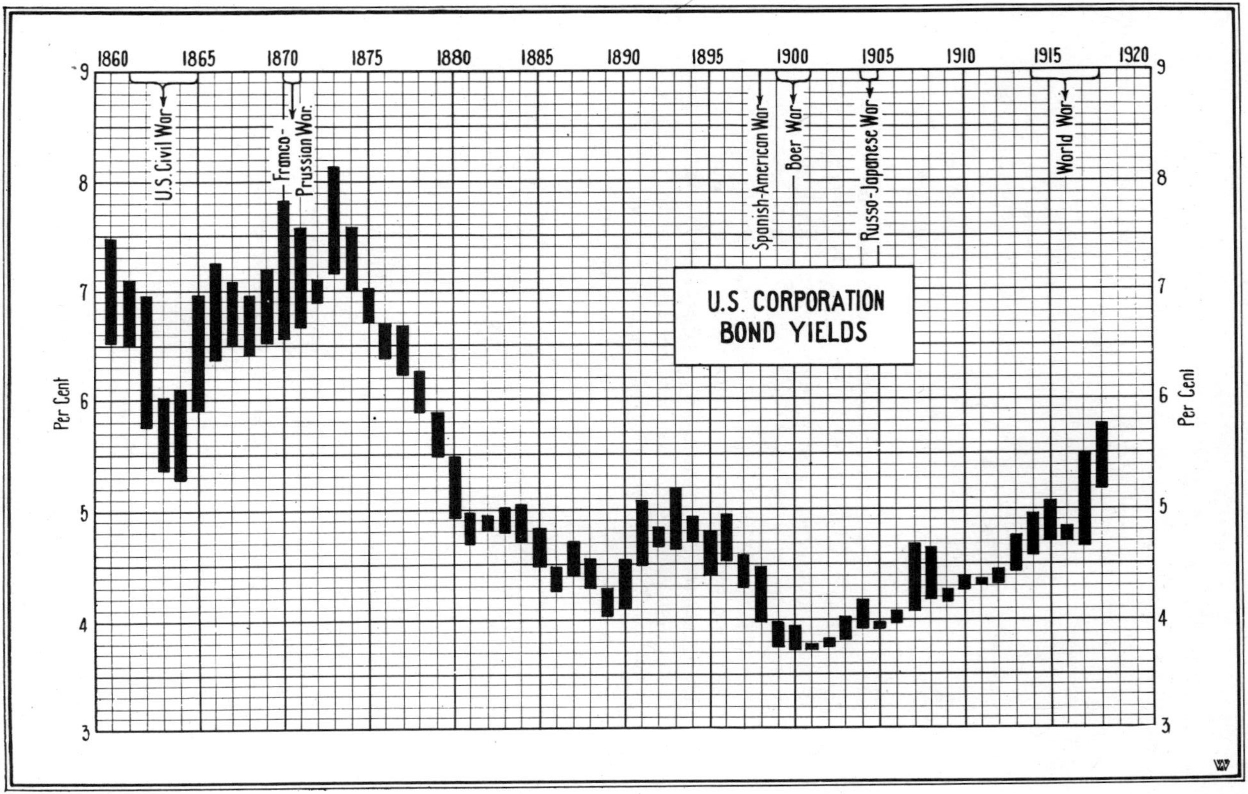
U.S. CORPORATION
BOND YIELDS
Per Cent
1860
1865
1870
1875
1880
1885
1890
1895
1900
1905
1910
1915
1920
3
4
5
6
7
8
9
U.S. Civil War
Franco-Prussian War
Spanish-American War
Boer War
Russo-Japanese War
World War

NOTATIONS TO CHARTS
ON PAGES 87 AND 89

**U.S. Corporation Bond Yields**
This graph is drawn from figures furnished by the Babson Statistical Organization. The bonds included were necessarily changed from time to time, but the net result is a pretty faithful reflection of corporation bond prices in the United States. It is necessary to show the yield rather than an average of bond prices because prices are affected by the maturity of the various bonds.

**U.S. Money Rates Prime Commercial Paper**
This graph is believed to be the first authentic record of money rates before 1870. The rates were compiled from the daily reports given by the newspapers of that time, a research involving a great deal of labor. Prime three to six months commercial paper was selected as a better reflection of actual conditions than call or time money, and it has the additional advantage of permitting earlier quotations. An effort was made to carry the graph back to the panic of 1837, but no adequate records were found before 1841. There were times in the late thirties when money was unobtainable at any rate. The evident scarcity of capital and the high rates obtained previous to 1873 shed an interesting light on our financial history.

**U.S. MONEY RATES PRIME COMMERCIAL PAPER**

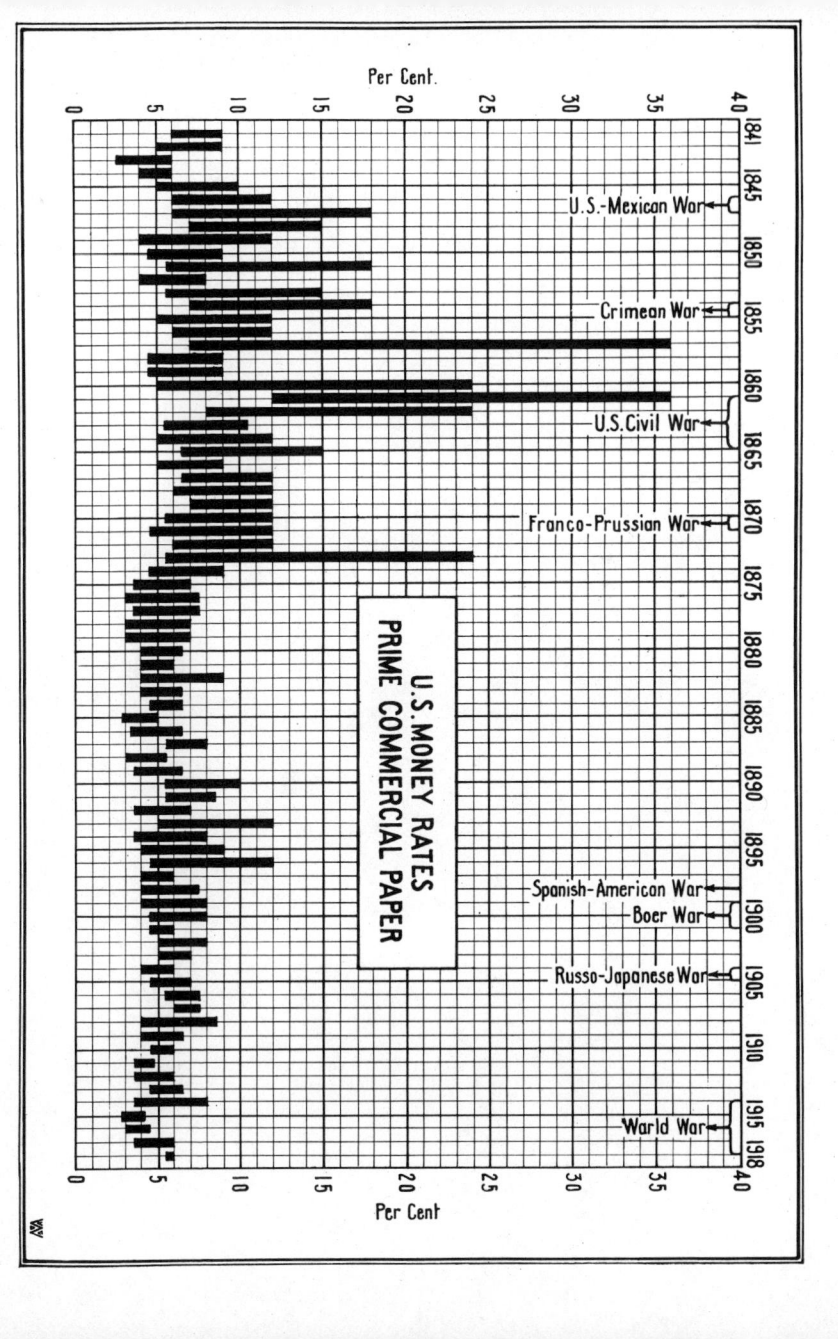

# CHAPTER V.

## PRINCIPLES OF STOCK PRICES
### By G. C. SELDEN

AT first glance the accompanying graph of stock prices since 1860 presents an appearance of lawless irregularity. But on further examination it proves to be one of the most interesting of the various graphs we have discussed.

First, what is the relation of stock prices to the other main factors discussed in preceding chapters?

Comparison with commodity prices (Chapter III) shows at once that there is no such general correspondence between stocks and commodities as we found to exist between bond yields and commodities.

# A CENTURY OF PRICES

Nevertheless a sharp rise in commodity prices has a strongly bullish influence on the stocks of companies which are free to advance the prices of their products in accordance with demand. In recent years this has not included railroads and public utilities; for while those companies have been granted advances in rates, the advances have not been sufficient to keep up with rising costs of operation.

## RISING COMMODITIES BENEFIT INDUSTRIALS

But owners of industrial stocks have benefited not only from the general inflationary effect of rising commodity prices, but they have also benefited further and very greatly *at the expense of bondholders.*

Suppose, for example, that an industrial company is capitalized at $300,000, of which $100,000 consists of 6 per cent bonds—making the annual interest charge $6,000—and

## A CENTURY OF PRICES

$200,000 is in the form of stock on which 6 per cent, or $12,000, is being earned annually. Now let us suppose that a great rise in commodity prices occurs, which doubles this company's cost of production and also doubles the selling price of its products. It is evident that its profits—in dollars—will also be doubled.

The bondholders do not share in this increased profit. Their return is fixed at $6,000. But the company's profits applicable to its securities have increased from $18,000 to $36,000. So $30,000 is now left for the stock, or 15 per cent on the $200,000 outstanding. And this without any change in the company's per cent of profit on its output.

This shows us one of the principal causes of the growth in the profits of industrial companies during the period of rising commodity prices which began with 1898, and

# A CENTURY OF PRICES

which from 1915 to 1918 was such a controlling factor in our whole economic life. The same principle must necessarily operate in any great advance in commodities, while a sharp decline in commodities will cut down the earnings on stocks with corresponding rapidity.

In the case of a company which, in addition to bonds, has preferred stocks on which the dividend return is limited to a fixed per cent, the effect on the earnings for the common stock is even more marked. If, as is sometimes the case, three-quarters of a company's earnings on a low-price basis were required for bonds and preferred stocks, a doubling of commodity prices should multiply the earnings for the common stock by five.

## PANICS AFFECT ALL SECURITIES

In comparing bond yields and money rates with stock prices, we see that panics,

## A CENTURY OF PRICES

even of a relatively minor character, affect all three. Bond and stock prices fall and money rates rise. The effect on bonds is temporary and in the case of minor panics unimportant.

The years of high money rates—1860, 1865, 1873, 1882, 1890, 1893, 1896, 1907, 1914—have also included a sharp fall in stocks, with the single exception of 1882. In that year the high rates were due to the constant absorption of money by the U. S. Treasury, rather than to general economic conditions.

On the other hand, there were considerable declines in stocks in 1884 and 1903 without much effect on commercial paper rates. In both cases the panicky conditions were practically confined to Wall Street, and call money was sharply affected— reaching 3 per cent a day in 1884*—but since commercial conditions were good,

---
* A few loans were reported as having been made at 5 per cent a day.

# A CENTURY OF PRICES

mercantile borrowers were able to postpone their requirements until the pinch in Wall Street was over.

## THE MINOR CYCLE

From the standpoint of general principles, the most interesting point connected with stock prices is the comparatively regular swing noticeable since 1884, which has come to be called "the minor cycle." An examination of the graph shows that low prices for stocks, accompanied in most cases (but not all) by relatively high money rates, have occurred every three or four years with an astonishing degree of regularity. These years have been as follows: 1884, 1887, 1890, 1893, 1896, 1900, 1903, 1907, 1910, 1914, 1917.

In between these low points there has been in each case an upward surge in stock prices. In most instances there have been about two years of rising prices and one

## A CENTURY OF PRICES

year of decline. The reason for this will appear later.

A regular swing of this character, occurring throughout such a long period, indicates the strong probability of some general law. And this probability is increased by the great variety of explanations advanced for the recurrent declines.

The panic of 1884 was alleged to be due to the Grant & Ward failure, accompanied by the collapse of the Marine Bank and followed by a few other bank failures. For the decline of 1887 only the most general reasons could be assigned, such as over-expansion, over-extension of mercantile credits, etc. The drop of 1890 was assumed to be the reflection on this side of the Baring failure in London.

The panic of 1893 was a mystery to current commentators. Later judgments have attributed it to a variety of reasons, of

## A CENTURY OF PRICES

which the Government's continued heavy coinage of silver and dwindling supply of gold perhaps carry the weight of the most authority. The decline of 1896 was immediately due to the fear that the pending election would result in a silver basis for our currency.

The low prices of 1900 were mostly confined to railroad stocks. The industrials were then feeling the benefit of rising commodity prices. The movement was generally considered a reaction from excessive speculation. The bear market of 1903 was labeled the "undigested securities panic," and thought to be due to the over-issue of industrial stocks.

In 1907 came a "money panic," again due to over-expansion. For the moderate decline of 1910 falling railroad earnings and the Government's intention to prosecute leading corporations under the Sherman anti-trust law were assigned as reasons. The low prices of 1913 were due to general depression and were followed by the war panic in 1914. The great decline of 1917 was in part due to our entrance into the war and the prospective great demands for capital for war purposes.

In nearly every instance over-expansion, over-extension of loans, over-speculation, or over-something-else, has been mentioned as one of the causes contributing to the decline. Is it not at least probable that these "overs" are the main cause of the minor cycle, and that the special events of the time are contributing factors which make greater or smaller a decline which would have occurred in any case?

## THE FUNDAMENTAL CAUSE

The fundamental cause of the minor cycle is the law of action and reaction, the building up process and the falling down process.

## A CENTURY OF PRICES

At low prices, stocks are mostly in the hands of courageous, outright investors, who cannot easily be frightened into selling. As prices rise, more and more stocks pass into the hands of buyers for profit only. The higher quotations go, the more the public comes into the market. Nothing so strongly stimulates speculative purchases as the spectacle of rising prices.

Buyers at high prices are necessarily of a weaker class—weaker in judgment and therefore weaker in resources—than buyers at low prices. After a prolonged and extensive advance, a great volume of stocks becomes lodged in the hands of these weak holders, while many of the stronger class of investors have realized at the high prices and transferred their funds into more stable securities, such as bonds or short term notes.

Eventually these weak speculative holders have bought all they want, or some of them become discouraged, or some unfavorable event dampens their ardor. They then begin to sell out on each other—since prices are too high to attract the genuine investor for income.

For such a situation there is no cure except a decline to a level which will attract the stronger class of buyers. So we next have the downward swing of the cycle. How far the fall must go depends mostly on the supply of liquid capital, which is roughly indicated by money rates.

During the rise, with the public active in the market, there is a great deal of shifting from one holder to another, accompanied by reactions, temporary slackening of activity, and renewed advances. Investors part with their holdings gradually, as each becomes satisfied with the prices to be obtained. But the decline consists mostly of

## A CENTURY OF PRICES

weak holders letting go to other weak holders. For that reason the fall is more rapid than the advance.

In the meantime much the same thing is occurring in many lines of industry. Speculation is by no means confined to stocks—"the instinct of anticipation" is general. Buyers of goods try to purchase not only at the cheapest place but very often at the cheapest *time* also. The bargain sale attracts the housewife because she believes the goods are cheaper than they were last week or may be next week. She is a speculator, though she doesn't realize it.

The morning newspaper would seem to be something which no one would try to buy at the cheapest time. Yet some commuters who have to pay an extra cent for a paper at their station buy only one to read on the train, waiting to buy another at the regular price in the city.

## A CENTURY OF PRICES

In the larger affairs of business, almost every purchaser tries to buy as far ahead as possible when he thinks prices will rise, and to delay buying as long as possible when he thinks they will fall. Rising prices, unless already very high, bring increased orders, but buying falls off on declining prices until it is believed that the bottom has been reached.

In this way the spirit of speculation, unrecognized, or at any rate not called by that name, permeates all business, and the minor cycle in a modified form is a feature of industry as well as of the stock market. Any chart of steel prices, unfilled steel orders, pig iron production, or bank clearings plainly shows the modifying effect of the cycle.

The importance of this in the present discussion lies in the mutual influence which the stock market and general business conditions exert upon each other. A widespread willingness to buy in any industry tends to increase its prosperity, for the time being. Its prosperity tends toward higher prices for the stocks of companies in the industry. And rising prices for the stocks tend to encourage business men to extend their undertakings—since many of them realize that the stock market, properly interpreted, is a valuable indicaion as to future conditions.

Each dog in a pack of hounds runs faster and longer because he sees the others running; and with all our intellectual development, this primary instinct remains. We catch each other's enthusiasm or depression. In any market where the spirit of speculation exists—and it would be hard to name any where it is wholly absent—rising prices once started tend to continue rising until they are obviously too high, and falling prices tend to fall until they are obviously low. And that is the main part of the story of the minor cycle.

### FEATURES OF THE MINOR CYCLE

The relation of money rates to the swing of stocks in the minor cycle is of interest, but is not so direct or decisive as might at first be thought. It has usually been the case after a bull movement in stocks, that when prime commercial paper at New York, after a period of lower rates, advanced to a 6 per cent basis, the advance in stock prices proved to be practically over. Then money has remained around the 6 per cent basis, or in some cases higher, during the downward swing of the stock cycle. After the completion of the liquidation in stocks, the money rate has usually dropped, within a few months, to around a 4 per cent. basis, or in some instances lower.

The highest money rate has corresponded

# A CENTURY OF PRICES

rather closely with the lowest prices for stocks, falling gradually as stocks began to rally, remaining for a time near a 4 per cent level, and then rising to 6 per cent as stocks reached their top. Theoretically, it might seem that the lowest money rate should correspond with the highest prices for stocks; but that is not the case, for speculation, once under way, carries stock prices upward even though the money rate rises at the same time.

Another reason why money rates and stock prices do not move more in harmony is because, so far as the demand for money is concerned, stock speculation is the tail to the kite—the kite being the money requirements of general business. When business really needs money, it takes it away from the stock market. A bull market in stocks is based on surplus funds, which at the time are not needed for other lines of business.

## A CENTURY OF PRICES

It would, however, be a mistake to suppose that the structure of a bull market will not topple over until the money rate rises sharply. It sometimes falls of its own weight, so to speak, while money remains cheap. This occurred in the autumn of 1916, when the highest prices for stocks were made on a 3 3-4 per cent rate for commercial paper, and the rate did not rise to 6 per cent until after the low prices of December, 1917, were past.

The Federal Reserve System, with its easy rediscounting, will prevent extremely high money rates and may have the effect of reducing the general average of rates somewhat. It will not, however, seriously reduce the supply of money available for stock market purposes as compared with the past. Nothing else is so mobile as credit. Loanable funds will seek the best rates as surely as water seeks its level.

The minor cycle in industry is more

## A CENTURY OF PRICES

clearly and promptly reflected in the unfilled orders of the U. S. Steel Corporation than in any other statistics now available. These follow the swings of the stock market quite regularly, keeping three to six months behind stocks at the high and low turns. For that reason the minor cycle in stocks is decidedly helpful in forecasting coming conditions in the steel industry, with which other trades also strongly sympathize.

NOTATIONS TO CHART<br>
ON PAGE 109

### Stock Prices

From 1860 to 1900 the average used is that of twenty railway stocks compiled by Henry Hall. From 1900 to 1912 the Dow-Jones twenty rails are used, the average having been substantially identical with Henry Hall's at the end of 1900. In more recent years the rails have not adequately represented the general course of the market, therefore we show the New York *Times* average of twenty-five rails and twenty-five industrials combined, which makes necessary a change of scale. These are believed to be the best averages available for the different periods. The fact should be noted, however, that the reduction of the scale for the years 1912 to 1918 has the effect of narrowing the fluctuations of that period somewhat as compared with the rest of the graph.

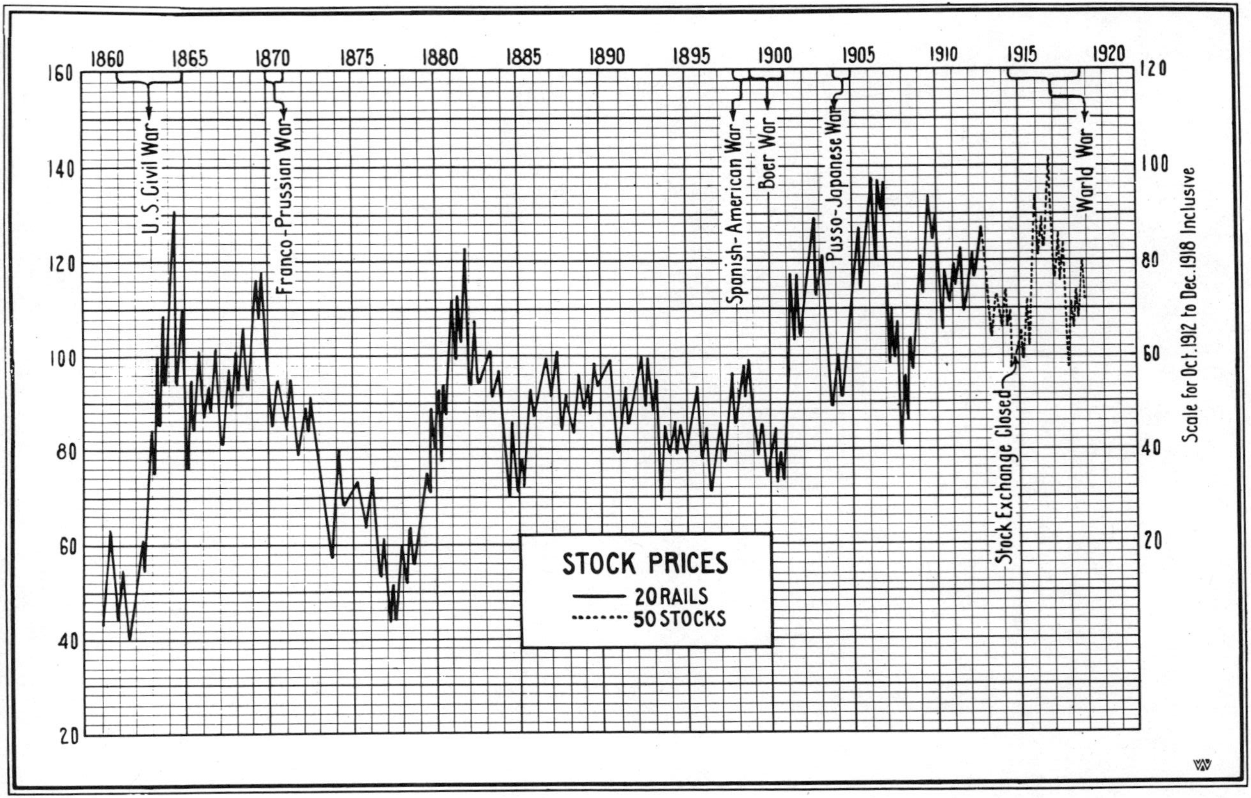
STOCK PRICES
20 RAILS
50 STOCKS
U.S. Civil War
Franco-Prussian War
Spanish-American War
Boer War
Pusso-Japanese War
Stock Exchange Closed
World War
1860
1865
1870
1875
1880
1885
1890
1895
1900
1905
1910
1915
1920
160
140
120
100
80
60
40
20
120
100
80
60
40
20
Scale for Oct. 1912 to Dec. 1918 Inclusive

# BIBLIOGRAPHY

**Adams, H. C.** Finance.
**Rabbeno, Ugo.** The American Commercial Policy.
**Bagehot, Walter.** Lombard Street.
**Baring, A. (Lord Ashburton).** The Financial and Commercial Crisis Considered.
**Bastable, Chas. F.** Theory of International
**Bastable, C. F.** Public Finance.
**Beveridge, N. H.** Unemployment: A Problem of Industry.
**Bilgram, H., & Levy, L.** Cause of Business Depressions as Disclosed by Analysis of the Basic Principles of Economics.
**Bogart, E. L.** Economic History of the U. S.
**Bogart, E. L.** Business Economics.
**Bowley, A. L.** The Effect of the War on the External Trade of the United Kingdom.
**Bowley, A. L.** The Elements of Statistics.
**Brace, H. H.** The Value of Organized Speculation.
**Brown, H. G.** International Trade and Exchange.
**Brown, J. B.** Causes of Business Depression.
**Browne, Scribner.** Tidal Swings of the Stock Market.

# A CENTURY OF PRICES

**Burton, Theodore E.** Financial Crises.
**Chaddock, Robert E.** State Banking Before the Civil War, and the Safety Fund Banking System in N. Y. State (U. S. 61st Congress, 2nd Session, Senate Doc. 5811).
**Chamberlain, Lawrence.** Principles of Bond Investment.
**Clare, George.** The A. B. C. of Exchange.
**Clare, George.** The Money Market Primer.
**Conant, C.** A History of Modern Banks of Issue with Account of Economic Crises of the 19th Century and Crisis of 1907.
**Copeland, Melvin T.** Business Statistics.
**Copeland, Melvin T.** Cotton Manufacturing Industry of U. S.
**Crowell, F.** How to Forecast Business and Investment Conditions.

**Daggett, Stuart.** Railroad Reorganizations.
**Davenport, H. J.** The Economics of Enterprise.
**De Launay, L.** The World's Gold.
**Dewey, David R.** Financial History of the U. S.
**Dewing, A. S.** Corporate Promotions and Reorganizations.
**Disbrow, C. W.** Periodic Financial Panics: The Cause and the Remedy.
**Dunbar, C. F.** Chapters on the Theory and History of Banking.
**Ely, R. T.** Monopolies and Trusts.

# A CENTURY OF PRICES

**Emery, H. C.**   Speculation on the Stock and Produce Exchanges of the U. S.
**Fisher, Irving.**   Why is the Dollar Shrinking? A Study in the High Cost of Living.
**Fisher, Irving.**   Nature of Capital and Income.
**Fisher, Irving.**   Rate of Interest: Its determination and relation to economic phenomena.
**Fisher, Irving.**   Purchasing Power of Money: Its determination and relation to credit, interest and crises.
**George, Henry.**   Progress and Poverty.
**Gibson, T. W.**   Cycles of Speculation.
**Giffen, Robert.**   Economic Inquiries and Studies.
**Hall, Henry.**   How Money is Made in Security Investments.
**Hawley, F. B.**   Enterprise and the Productive Process.
**Hickernell, N. F.**   Methods of Business Forecasting Based on Fundamental Statistics.
**Higginson, J. L.**   Tariffs at Work.
**Hirst, W.**   The Political Economy of War.
**Hobson, John A.**   Gold, Prices and Wages, with an Examination of the Quantity Theory.
**Hobson, John A.**   Causes of the Rise in Prices (U. S. 62nd Congress, 3rd Session, Senate Doc. 980).
**Hobson, J. A.**   Evolution of Modern Capitalism.

# A CENTURY OF PRICES

**Hull, G.**   High Prices and Industrial Depressions.

**Hyndman, H. M.**   Commercial Crises of the 19th Century.

**Jevons, W. C.**   Investigations in Currency and Finance.

**Jevons, H. S.**   Essays in Economics.

**Jevons, W. S.**   Money and the Mechanism of Exchange.

**Johnson, E. R., and Huebner, G. G.**   Railroad Traffic and Rates (2 volumes).

**Jones, E. D.**   Economic Crises.

**Juglar, C.**   Brief History of Panics and Their Periodical Occurrence in the U. S.

**Kemmerer, Edwin W.**   Money and Credit: Instruments in Their Relation to General Prices.

**Kemmerer, Edwin W.**   Seasonal Variations in the Relative Demand for Money and Capital in the U. S.   (U. S. 61st Congress 2nd Session, Senate Doc. 588.)

**Kinley, David.**   Money and Currency.

**Kinley, David.**   Use of Credit Instruments in Payments in the U. S. (U. S. 61st Congress 2nd Section, Senate Doc. 339.)

**Lauck, W. J.**   Causes of the Panic of 1893.

**Laughlin, James L.**   The Principles of Money.

**Laughlin, James L.**   Money and Prices.

**Laughlin, James L.**   Suggestions for Banking Reform.

# A CENTURY OF PRICES

**Layton, W. T.** Introduction to the Study of Prices with Special Reference to the 19th Century.
**Lyons, W. H.** Corporation Finance (Complete Edition).
**Margraff, A. W.** International Exchange.
**Marshall, Alfred.** Principles of Economics.
**Mayo-Smith, Richard.** Statistics and Economics.
**Mitchell, W. C.** Gold, Prices and Wages under the Greenback Standard, 1862-1880.
**Mitchell, W. C.** History of the Greenbacks, with Special Reference to Economic Consequences of their Issue.
**Mitchell, W. C.** Business Cycles.
**Moore, H. L.** Economic Cycles: Their Law and Cause.
**Moore, H. L.** Forecasting the Yield and Price of Cotton.
**Noyes, Alfred.** Forty Years of American Finance.
**Pratt, S. S.** The Work of Wall Street.
**Perrin, J.** Trade Fluctuations and Panics.
**Raffalovich, A.** Les Crises Commerciales et financières depuis 1889.
**Ripley, W. Z.** Railroads: Rates and Regulation—Volume I. Railroads: Finance and Organization—Volume II.
**Rodbertus, J. K.** Overproduction and Crises.
**Selden, G. C.** Psychology of the Stock Market.

# A CENTURY OF PRICES

**Selden, G. C.**   Investing for Profit.
**Selden, G. C.**   A. B. C. of Bond Buying.
**Smart, William.**   Studies in Economics.
**Smart, William.**   Distribution of Wealth.
**Sprague, Ezra.**   The Accountancy of Investments.
**Sprague, O. M.**   History of Crises under the National Banking System.
**Streighthoff, F. H.**   The Standard of Living Among the Industrial People of America.
**Streighthoff, F. H.**   The Distribution of Incomes. Columbia University, Studies in History, Economics and Public Law, Vol. III, No. 2.
**Taussig, F. W.**   Tariff History of the U. S. Trade.
**Van Hise, C. R.**   Concentration and Control.
**Veblen, Thornstein B.**   Theory of Business Enterprise.
**Walker, Francis, Amasa.**   Discussion in Economics and Statistics—Edited by David R. Dewey.
**Walker, Francis, Amasa.**   Money in Its Relation to Trade and Industry.
**Walsh, C. M.**   The Measurement of General Exchange Value: The Fundamental Problem of Monetary Science.
**Webb, Sidney and Beatrice.**   History of Trade Unionism.
**Webb, Sidney and Beatrice.**   Industrial Democracy.

# A CENTURY OF PRICES

**Weld, L. D. H.** The Marketing of Farm Products.
**Wells, David A.** Recent Economic Changes and their Effect on Production and Distribution of Wealth and Well-being of Society.
**Withers, Hartley.** Stocks and Shares.
**Withers, Hartley.** Money Changing.
**Withers, Hartley.** The Meaning of Money.
**Zartman, L. U.** The Investments of Life Insurance Companies.

————. Annual Report—Comptroller of the Currency.

————. Annual Report—Director of the Mint.

————. Annual Report—Federal Reserve Board.

————. Annual Report—Treasurer of the U. S.

————. Bulletins of United States Department of Labor.

————. Cotton Facts. Edited by Geller, C.

————. Federal Reserve Bulletin (Monthly) Federal Reserve Board.

————. History of Prices During the War (1914-1918), Price Section, War Industries Board—Edited by W. C. Mitchell.

————. Metal Statistics—Published by the American Metal Market Company.

————. Monthly Summary of Foreign

# A CENTURY OF PRICES

Commerce of the U. S.
———. National Monetary Commission Publications.
———. Readings in the Economics of the War—Edited by J. Maurice Clark, Walton H. Hamilton and Harold C. Moulton.
———. Reports of the American Iron and Steel Institute.
———. Report on Cotton Exchanges—Commissioner of Corporations.
———. Reports of the Department of Agriculture.
———. Report of United States Industrial Commission.
———. Special Census Reports on Wealth, Debt and Taxation.
———. Statistical Abstract of the U. S.
———. The Making and Using of Index Numbers (Bulletin of U. S. Department of Labor, No. 173).